CREATURES OF PARADISE

Bryan Holme

CREATURES OF PARADISE

Pictures to Grow Up With

Oxford University Press

New York and Toronto

The Garden of Eden. Erastus Salisbury Field. American, 1805–1900

Frontispiece. *Raven Addressing Assembled Animals*. Indian, Mughal School, c. 1590

Library of Congress Cataloging in Publication Data
Holme, Bryan, 1913–
   Creatures of Paradise
   Summary: through a selection of 117 illustrations, explores the depiction of animals by artists throughout the ages
   1. Animals in art–Juvenile literature
   2. Art–Juvenile literature
   (1. Animals in art.   2. Art appreciation.)   I. Title
N 7660.   H643 704.9'432   80–10867
ISBN 0–19–520205–8

Filmset in Great Britain by Keyspools Ltd, Golborne, Lancs
Printed and bound in Japan by Dai Nippon

'I think I could turn and live with animals,
They are so placid and self-contained.'

Walt Whitman (*Song of Myself*)

On the opposite page:
The American 'primitive' painter,
Erastus Salisbury Field, based this
painting of Adam and Eve
surrounded by animals and birds,
on an illustration by the English
artist, John Martin. Hardly to be
noticed in the middle of the
Garden of Eden is the evil serpent
who, after tempting Eve to pick
the forbidden apple, slithers away
to the left of the tree.

The earliest garden, described in the Old Testament as lying 'eastward in Eden', is known also as the 'Garden of Delights', 'Garden of God', and in later Christian writings, 'Garden of Paradise'.

In visualizing the Paradise which Adam and Eve shared 'with every beast of the field and every fowl of the air', artists have often given more attention to the beauty of Eden, and to the wild creatures living at peace with each other, than to Adam and Eve.

The same idea, developed later in the Old Testament, of an earthly paradise to come, in which not only 'the wolf shall dwell with the lamb', but all animals live in perfect harmony, so impressed the American folk artist, Edward Hicks, that he kept painting *The Peaceable Kingdom* over and over again until he had made nearly a hundred versions of it. Two of these numerous surviving examples appear on pages 8–9.

Although the remaining pictures depart from this idyllic theme, it serves most suitably to introduce the work as a whole. Intended not only as a book of animals but also as an introduction to art, particularly for young readers, *Creatures of Paradise* aims to present, as an exhibition in an art museum might, a collection of drawings, paintings and sculptures of beautiful animals and birds that have been portrayed lovingly, as well as skilfully, by great artists of all countries and centuries.

That less fortunate aspects of nature exist must be acknowledged, yet animals painted 'in savage chase, or butchered agony', as John Ruskin put it, would be out of place in a book of pictures to grow up with.

The subjects follow a more or less logical progression, beginning with the Bible scenes and leading into individual pictures of wild animals – the elephant, camel, lion and monkey, for instance – then moving on to farm animals, horses, dogs and cats, and finally, after a flight of birds, to fantastic creatures and animals in literature. Yet the book is so planned that it can be picked up, set aside and returned to by readers of any age, at any page.

'And whatsoever Adam called every living creature, that was the name thereof.' William Blake's interpretation of the naming of the animals shows Adam pointing to the good animals with his right hand while pressing the evil serpent down with his left.

The story of Noah rounding up all the creatures to be saved from the flood is, like the Garden of Eden, one of the most difficult subjects an artist can choose because of the many different animals he must paint. The sixteenth-century artist, Jacopo Bassano, nearly always included animals in his landscapes, but he and his assistants outdid themselves here with the long and harmonious procession which winds its way toward the Ark. At the end of the gangplank Noah is on hand to receive the animals – two by two.

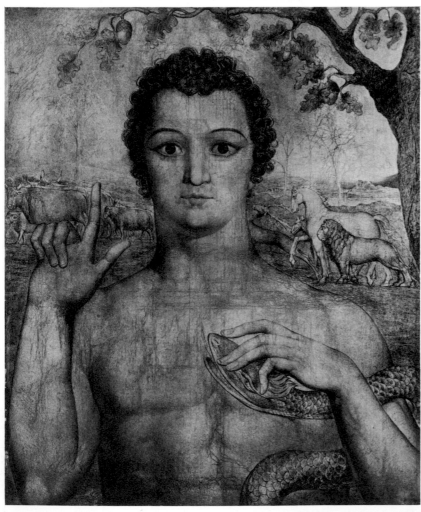

Adam Naming the Beasts. William Blake. English, 1757–1827

The Animals Going into the Ark (detail). Studio of Jacopo Bassano. Italian, 16th cent.

The Peaceable Kingdom. Edward Hicks. American, 1780–1849

Here are two variations of *The Peaceable Kingdom*, which the self-taught painter, Edward Hicks, based on the passage in Isaiah that reads:
'The wolf shall dwell with the lamb and the leopard shall lie down with the kid, the calf and the young lion...together, and a little child shall lead them. And the cow and the bear shall feed; their young ones shall lie down together, and the lion shall eat straw like the ox.'

As a devoted Quaker, Hicks also prayed that people should live together in peace and, in the picture above, pointedly included the scene at left, adapted from a painting by Benjamin West. In it we see William Penn making a peace treaty with Indians for the land on which the city of Philadelphia was to be built.

The Peaceable Kingdom (detail), 1830
Edward Hicks. American, 1780–1849

ISAIAH 11 Chap.

A Camel with his Driver. Attributed to Sultan Muhammed. Persian, mid-16th cent.

'A camel's all lumpy', C. E. Curry's poem goes, 'and bumpy and humpy.' But in that lump nature cleverly stores the fat the camel needs to carry him across the waterless desert. This well-groomed 'ship of the desert' is led forward to the jingle of ankle bells.

The cheetah is such a fast cat it can outstrip every other animal over short distances. When this drawing was made, it was also known that the cheetah had certain dog-like characteristics: notably blunt claws, the inability to climb trees, and a reasonable willingness to be tamed and trained for hunting – hence the collar and chains.

Cheetahs. Italian, Lombard School, 15th cent.

Many thousands of years ago, when our ancestors still lived in caves, the first pictures they drew were of animals, frequently with themselves in pursuit. The prehistoric engraving of a giraffe and an elephant, opposite, was found on a rock in Fezzan, North Africa.

A water buffalo cast in bronze. In ancient China where it was made, the water buffalo, or ox, symbolized masculine strength.

Water Buffalo. Chinese, Chou Dynasty, c. 10th cent. BC

Giraffe and Elephant. North Africa, after 3000 BC

The Sleeping Gypsy. Henri Rousseau. French, 1844–1910

The king of beasts, crowned, as in England's national emblem, was once a familiar tavern sign in Colonial America too. But after the American War of Independence had been won, not only did the lion lose its crown, but in 1818 a Connecticut sign artist carried things a step further when he presented a Hartford inn keeper with this disgruntled looking Leo in chains.

Goodwin Tavern Sign, c. 1818. William Rice. American, 1773–1847

Henri Rousseau's famous lion with an eye as round as the moon, who stands and stares and sniffs at the sleeping gypsy, drew more smiles than it did praise from critics when the painting was first shown in Paris in 1897. While no one thought to buy such a 'bewildering, naive' painting then, the popularity and value of this masterpiece today is beyond anything Rousseau would have imagined even in his wildest dreams. Pleased with what he had done, Rousseau explained: 'the feline, though ferocious, hesitates to pounce upon its prey, who, exhausted, has fallen into a deep sleep' – leaving us little the wiser, perhaps, but delighted just the same.

Elephant. Artist unknown. Chinese, Chou Dynasty, 1122–249 BC

'When people call the beast in mind,
They marvel more and more
At such a little tail behind
So LARGE a trunk before.'

Hilaire Belloc (*The Elephant*)

No likeness of the elephant could be more charmingly out of the ordinary than this two- to three-thousand-year-old bronze wine vessel from China. The tiny elephant, duplicating the expression of surprise on the big elephant's face, serves very practically as the handle of the lid.

It looks like a charming toy elephant here, but in reality it is a life-size model. The enormous frame of heavy wire with realistic tusks and toes was specially made to display an elephant's trappings.

Elephant Armour. Indian, used at Battle of Plessy, 1757

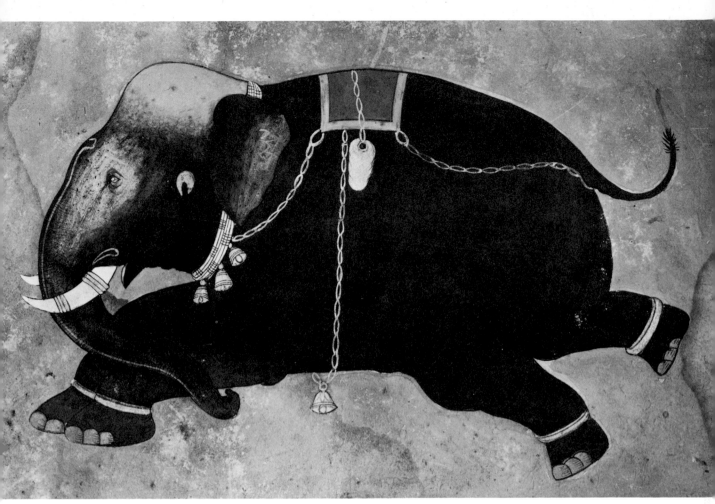

Escaping Elephant. Indian, Rajasthan, c. 1800

Even to elephants there must be times when the
grass looks greener on the other side of the fence.
Who knows but this escaping elephant has his own
ideas, or memories, of some beauteous spot lying far,
far beyond the grounds of the Maharaja's palace –
and to this paradise he is now headed full tilt.

Bear in a Tree. American, c. 1850

The bear is too big for the tree, of course, but in folk art, proportion, perspective, and the laws of gravity become matters of passing consequence. Not only did this artist neglect to leave enough room for the bear without tilting the stencil in a way he never intended, but he was obviously too proud of the

Mao Mao the Giant Panda, c. 1939. Chiang Yee. Chinese, 20th cent.

stag to change its smile to an expression of alarm – or its walk to a leap – which would have been logical with a tiger so close behind. But this is all part of the painting's charm.

This illustration from the story 'Chin-Pao and the Giant Pandas' is of the enchanting giant panda, Mao-Mao, with whom a five-year-old boy, Chin Pao, lived. In contrast to the stencilled *Bear in a Tree*, Chiang Tee's aim was to paint as realistic and exquisite a picture as he possibly could.

Three Koalas, 1957. Edward John Stevens. American, b. 1923

Left: Bears, this fifteenth-century Persian artist firmly tells us, can be just as determined as anyone else. This is a bear that gets there! Realizing, through instinct perhaps, that their mother might have walked off and left them for ever to fend for themselves – as mother bears eventually do – the cubs at the bottom of the tree look much less certain of the big wide world than the one on his way to the top.

Three Bear Cubs. Persian, early 15th cent.

To bring an animal convincingly alive in a drawing or painting is difficult enough, but to chisel a likeness out of stone is, of course, that much harder. At right, Heinz Warnecke has captured the very essence of two bears at play.

Tumbling Bears. Heinz Warnecke. American, 20th cent.

The most popular haunt of the soft and pudgy koala, or Australian native bear, is the gum tree, or eucalyptus, where it climbs to play delightfully, sleep by day, and gather flowers and leaves to eat at night.

The fox squirrel is the largest squirrel in the United States and the most interesting, said America's great naturalist, John James Audubon. While drawing the jolly pair above, Audubon noted in his Journal: 'At times it [the fox squirrel] takes possession of the hole of the ivory-billed woodpecker. The wood duck is frequently in competition for the same residence, and contests take place. The male and female duck unite in chasing and beating with their wings any squirrel that may approach their nests, nor are they idle with their beaks and tongues. On the other hand, when the squirrel has its young in the hole of a tree and is intruded upon, it immediately rushes to the hole, enters it, protrudes its head occasionally and with a low angry bark keeps possession until the intruder wearies of the contest. Thus nature imparts to each species additional spirit and vigor in defence of its young.'

At right, a pair of red squirrels pause like ballet dancers on a bending bough. Beloved in Europe, even in England where the invasion of the American grey squirrel has made them an ever rarer sight, these agile creatures glide gracefully hither and yon selecting acorns, pine seeds and leaf buds to store – sometimes so far afield that they forget wherever in the world they could possibly have hidden them.

Fox Squirrels. John James Audubon. American, 1785–1851

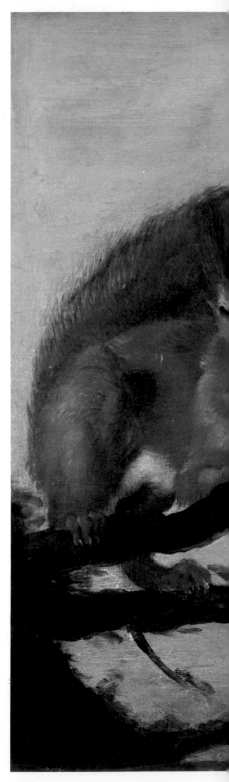

Squirrels on a Branch. Flemish, 17th cent.

Hare. Albrecht Dürer. German, 1471–1528

Rabbit with Figs. Wallpainting from Herculaneum, Italian, before AD 79

One of the most famous animal drawings of all time is Albrecht Dürer's study of a hare, a creature that is larger than a rabbit, has bigger ears, and longer legs that help it to be up and away faster in the face of danger. Dürer's drawing is so realistic you can almost feel the fur and see the nose twitch.

Rabbits even in Roman times were not just hunted, but loved – or so it would seem from the tender way this one was painted. Occupying a corner of a wall in Herculaneum before the volcano erupted and buried the city in AD 79, happily the little rabbit with the figs reappeared when excavations began some seventeen hundred years later.

Drawn with equal sympathy is Henri Matisse's field patterned with rabbits, opposite. Light, airy and frolicsome, the drawing sings of springtime and the advent of Easter.

Rabbits (detail). Henri Matisse. French, 1869–1954.

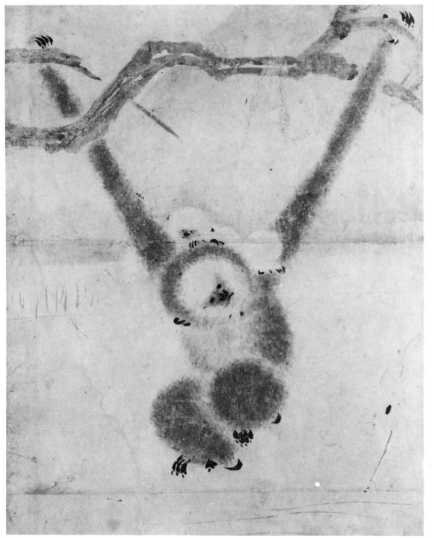

Monkeys and Birds in Trees (detail). Sesshu. Japanese, 1420–1506

Monkeys in Fruit Tree. Kawanabe Kiosai. Japanese, 19th cent.

Chimpanzee. John B. Flannagan. American, 1898–1942

'Though he endeavour all he can,
An ape will never be a man.'

George Withers (*First Lottery*)

Or, as others have put it, 'man can always be more like a monkey than a monkey can be like a man.' With arms stretched like ropes from a tree, a mother gives a young monkey a swing. The composition here is so perfect, the outlining of the monkey so subtle, the little brush strokes that denote the eyes, nose, mouth, ears and feet so crisp and correctly placed that this detail from a large painting by Sesshu becomes a little masterpiece of its own.

The sculptor, John Flannagan, saw in the natural form of stone what we see now – a hunched-up chimpanzee with head resting on knees. To help the stone become still more like a monkey he developed and smoothed the head a little, and added the fewest possible lines to indicate arms and legs.

It would seem that monkeys have been drawn more often and with more love, deftness and sense of fun by Japanese artists than by those of any other country. The branch having broken before he firmed up on the fruit, a monkey's pleasure turns to very human-looking anger. The next stop for these two is the ground.

26

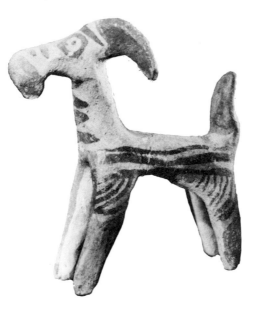

In Greece, where the green cow-pastures of northern Europe give way to hot dry lands and rocky mountains, the goat is greatly valued for its milk from which feta cheese can be made. This terracotta goat, as modern-looking as a ceramic by Picasso, was made nearly three thousand years ago.

Goat Statuette. Greek, Cyprus, 9th–8th cent. BC

The Persian wild goat, or pasang, is famous for its large backward-curving, scimitar-shaped horns. And, like all goats, it is noted for its sureness of foot while climbing rocky trails to the mountains. However, slips *do* occur, even in the best of families!

Falling Mountain Goat. Persian, 13th cent.

Most weathervanes spinning atop the old New England churches, houses, and barns, were shaped as horses, cows, pigs, cocks, ships, whales, or Indians shooting arrows. But here, in a rare example from Massachusetts, is a not-unfriendly-looking goat. It is made of wood, as some early vanes were, rather than of metal which came to be used almost exclusively.

Goat Weathervane. American, c. 1850–75

27

Woman Standing beside a Pool. Todi Ragini.
Indian, Rajasthan, *c.* 1725

Bahram Gur and Azada Just Before the Hunt.
Indian, Mughal School, *c.* 1595

Among the noblest of the wild animals, and perhaps the most universally loved for its beauty, is the deer. A hundred or more species, from red deer to reindeer, from wapiti to musk deer, are found all over the world. Some of the most exquisite illustrations of these graceful creatures appear with other animals in illuminated (or decorated) manuscripts of India and Persia.

Above is an eighteenth-century miniature of birds and deer with a lady by a pool, and opposite is a sixteenth-century painting of an Indian prince surrounded by animals in Paradise.

Although the bull was among the first wild animals to be exploited by man, in certain ancient civilizations this powerful beast of burden was also held sacred, as the cow is in India to this day. Images of the bull symbolized life, fire and fertility. The imperious creature seen here, in glistening silver touched with gold, is the top of a fourth-century BC rhyton, or horn-shaped drinking vessel, found in the part of Thrace that is now Bulgaria.

Bull Rhyton. Thracian, early 4th cent. BC

The American buffalo, or bison, still to be seen roaming western reservations, is a link that connects us with larger animals now extinct. Even as late as the 1830s and 1840s in America, herds of buffalo were dense enough to blacken the great prairies. The handsome buffalo bull, at left, was drawn by a folk artist, L. W. Frink, in 1871.

The Buffalo of the Plains. L. W. Frink. American, 19th cent.

Considering the brief life of a bowl in the average household, it seems little short of miraculous that this one from Cyprus could have lasted for over three thousand years. The design shows that bulls' habits haven't changed much through the centuries.

Bull and Bird. Pottery bowl. Greek, Cyprus, c. 1250 BC

John James Audubon, who painted the fox squirrels on p. 20, also made this sketch of a two-month-old buffalo calf at Fort George during his journey to the Missouri headwaters in 1843. One day, between daylight and noon, he sighted more than two thousand buffalo on the left bank of the river in what is now Lyman County, South Dakota.

Head of a Buffalo Calf, 1843. John James Audubon. American, 1785–1851

Although Egyptians living four thousand years ago left pictures of their farm animals, and European artists sometimes included animals and farms as details in religious paintings and illuminated manuscripts, it wasn't really until the seventeenth century in Europe that the romantic pastoral farm scene became a popular subject in itself. Everything about Rubens' painting of the peaceful farm at Laeken suggests beauty, harmony, and abundance.

The Farm at Laeken. Peter Paul Rubens. Flemish, 1577–1640

An Italian family is so taken up with the beautiful young calf that, for now at least, he seems assured of getting everything his heart desires. The artist, Filippo Palizzi, has cleverly based his composition on two imaginary triangles, the larger triangle taking in the calf with the three figures, the lesser triangle the calf's head and the two children at left.

In this seventeenth-century painting we enter a poultry yard on the grounds of a Dutch nobleman's estate, to find Jacoba, the ten-year-old daughter of the Baron of Wassenaar, feeding her pet lamb while posing for her portrait. The artist, Jan Steen, enjoyed suggesting that the longer pretty Jacoba paid attention to being painted, the less milk there would be for her lamb and the more there would be for the lucky dog to lap from the floor.

The Poultry Yard (detail). Jan Steen. Dutch, 1625/6–79

The Calf, 1859. Filippo Palizzi. Italian, 1818–99

Monsieur Juniet's Carriage. Henri Rousseau. French, 1844–1910

Pageant Sleigh, Representing a Stag Hunt. From the Nuremberg Tournament Book. German, 16th cent.

Besides domesticating the horse and harnessing it, we have been clever at coaxing other animals – even sheep – into pulling us along too. Fair enough, perhaps, when the animal is sufficiently loved to enjoy putting its best foot forward. And then how much prettier it usually turns out to be than the load in tow. No one seated in the cart, at left, rivals the charm of the pony. A very important member of the French family in Henri Rousseau's masterpiece is the tiny little dog stepping ahead. The pony is looking down at him behind blinkers.

The Young Aristocrat. Nicholas Winfield Scott-Leighton. English, 19th cent.

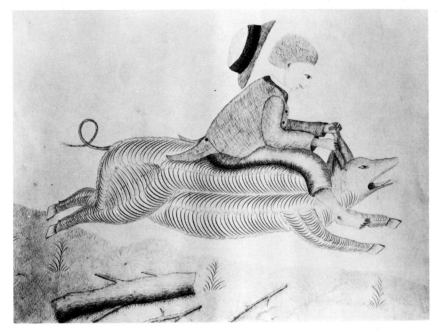

The boy's clothing immediately tells us that that this piggy-back was run much longer ago than anyone could possibly remember. To be more precise, it was in the 1860s, a time when steel-tipped pens were handed out in the classroom for 'copy-book' exercises. Students became so good at flourishing the pen for fancy script writing that practice strokes gave rise to doodles, and in turn to calligraphic drawings like this spirited example from Pennsylvania.

Pig Toy. Joseph Remmick. American, c. 1875

'He keeps a parlour boarder of a pig.'

Thomas Hood
(*The Irish Schoolmaster*)

'We do not allow him time for his education,' said Samuel Johnson of the pig in 1784, 'we kill him at a year old.' Perhaps, on the opposite page, the American artist Peggy Bacon was suggesting the living-room as a good place to make amends and friends with the pig; perhaps a recent caller had reminded her of one, or perhaps she simply wanted an excuse to draw a pig in a prettier setting than a sty? Her title, *The Ineluctable* (Unavoidable) *Caller*, leaves us to imagine anything we please.

The Ineluctable Caller. Peggy Bacon. American, b. 1895.

The solid little pig at left was carved out of wood, then lovingly smoothed and brushed with paint by a New Hampshire cobbler a little over one hundred years ago.

Below is the masterly way the American sculptor, Alexander Calder, outlined a pig in the air with wire. At once it leaves nothing, yet everything, to one's delighted imagination.

Sow. Alexander Calder. American, 1898–1976

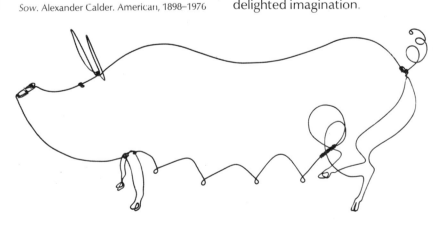

In most countries and in all centuries, the horse has been more generally useful and, with the exception of the dog, closer to man than any other animal. The splendid procession at right is a detail from a fourteenth-century Chinese manuscript, *Eighteen Songs of a Nomad Flute,* which retells the ancient tale of Lady Wen-Chi who was taken captive to Mongolia, later to be rescued and to return to her beloved China. Here the heroine is seen riding a dappled horse and wearing a wide hat with a veil. Behind the mounted flagbearers are two musicians on horseback playing flutes.

Departure from China. Chinese, Ming Dynasty, late 14th cent.

40

Horse. Antonio Pisanello. Italian, 1395–1455/6

A very early Greek krater, or vase, from Cyprus shows a surprised-looking horse yoked to a chariot. Were it not recorded that chariot horses were driven by the ancients in pairs, if not fours, it might be asked why there are four pairs of legs with what seems to be but one body.

The most difficult way to draw a horse is directly from the front or back. Pisanello made the two studies of the same horse, opposite, for his painting *St George and the Princess*, in the church of Sant'Anastasia in Verona.

Chariot (detail from krater). Greek, Cyprus, 1400–1375 BC

From chariots to carts to carriages: for centuries the horse was the prime mover of wheels. Constantin Guys, an eloquent recorder of fashionable nineteenth-century France, sketched the four-in-hand below, long before automobiles began their invasion of the highways, to send carriages like this elegant calash on their way to the museum.

The Calash. Constantin Guys. French, 1802–92

The Polish Rider. Rembrandt van Rijn. Dutch, 1606–69

Head of a White Horse. Théodore Géricault. French, 1791–1824

Rembrandt's haunting painting of a youth and horse journeying into the twilight. Both are framed by the distant cliff, at the foot of which lies a dark lake with a small fire showing dimly at the water's edge.

Few, if any, artists loved horses more passionately or drew them more often than the romantic French artist, Théodore Géricault. He painted this classic head when he was a young man of about twenty.

Some of the most ancient and beautiful sculptures of the horse come to us from Greece – usually in fragmentary form, however, like this magnificent marble chariot horse, once part of a team of four ornamenting a vast tomb at Halikarnassos.

By turning this old Persian puzzle all the way round and looking at it closely, four horses can be made out of the two heads and four pairs of legs. Two horses are facing, two are back to back.

Colossal Marble Horse (fragment). Greek, 4th cent. BC

Four Horses: Concentric Design. Persian, early 17th cent.

Princes – like the seventeenth-century Indian opposite – have always taken a special pride in their skill at riding. As an English writer of the same period, Ben Jonson, put it: 'Princes learn no art truly, but the art of horsemanship. The reason is, the brave beast is no flatterer. He will throw a Prince as soon as his groom.'

Equestrian Portrait of a Prince. Indian, Mughal School, 1627–58

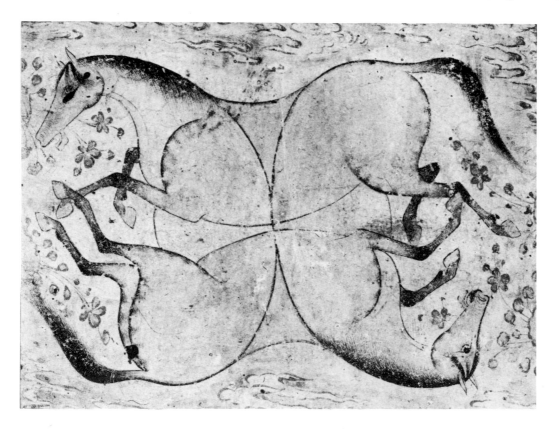

Any discussion of horses and English art leads inevitably to George Stubbs, whose book *The Anatomy of the Horse*, with his own illustrations, was published in 1766. But besides being a great painter of animals, Stubbs was a superb portrait and landscape artist, as this masterpiece in the Queen's collection shows. The Prince of Wales to whom this fine carriage, a phaeton, belonged was to become the Prince Regent, and later King George IV. The name of the coachman was Thomas, and the dog was called Fino.

Prince of Wales's Phaeton. George Stubbs. English, 1724–1806

'What good can it do an ass to be called a lion?'

Thomas Fuller (*Gnomologia*)

An unusual Roman mosaic found in Tunisia shows two plump lion cubs being nursed by a donkey whose expression clearly tells the way she feels.

Donkey Nursing Lion Cubs. Roman, Tunisia, 5th cent. AD

In contrast to Stubbs' formal and beautiful painting of a horse and phaeton, on the last two pages, is Doris Lee's informal portrait of a mare and two colts, at left. The meeting of the trunk of the tree with the neck of the mare as she reaches up to nibble the apple creates a perfect frame for the sprightly scene our eyes keep returning to – a mule colt showing how well she can kick.

Mare with Mule Colts. Doris Lee. American, 20th cent.

Edgar Degas has always been known for his paintings of the ballet, but this French Impressionist made nearly eighty sculptures as well. One of the liveliest of these is the rearing horse, at right, which he first sketched from life, then executed in wax before sending it to a foundry where it was cast in bronze.

Rearing Horse. Edgar Degas. French, 1834–1917

51

'Oh for a horse with wings!'

William Shakespeare (*Cymbeline*)

This is Pablo Picasso's drop curtain for the ballet, *Parade*, which was first danced by the Diaghilev company in Paris in 1917. The entertainment was described as a 'ballet of simplicity and fantasy in which Picasso gives us his own version of a fairground sideshow'. The curtain introduces a winged horse, like Pegasus in the Greek legend, an acrobat, a guitarist, a harlequin, and a dog.

Carved in 1880 to ride up and down on a 'merry-go-round' in Rhode Island, this spirited white carousel horse with green, brown, grey and orange trimmings has become a treasured example of the horse in popular art.

Carousel Horse. Henry Murphy (after carving by Charles Louff). American, c. 1880

Drop-curtain for 'Parade' (detail). Pablo Picasso. Spanish, 1881–1973

Henri de Toulouse-Lautrec was brought up in the country and loved animals, especially horses and dogs, which he made a practice of sketching. One of his greatest childhood thrills was being taken to see the horses at the circus. Never was he to tire of this form of entertainment which he grew up to view as 'an ideal spectacle because it is both realistic and imaginative'. The definition might apply equally to his sketch on the opposite page which shows a clown with a pony and monkey at one of the circuses he frequented in Paris. The baboon's big act was to jump on the pony's back and ride round and round the ring.

Clown, Pony and Monkey Rider.
Henri de Toulouse-Lautrec. French, 1864–1901

Lautrec is quoted as having said that he never drew 'a distinct frontier' between men and animals. This could well explain the expression on the face of the dog, Follette, which looks so human.

Follette. Henri de Toulouse-Lautrec. French, 1864–1901

The spirited impression of a horse and carriage below comes from the sketchbook Lautrec started at the age of sixteen. This was a year or so after the great tragedy of his life when he was crippled as the result of a bone disease.

Woman Driving a Carriage and Pair.
Henri de Toulouse-Lautrec. French, 1864–1901

A small face at the edge of the world. The dog's master, the artist Francisco de Goya, once remarked that when he wasn't painting portraits at the Spanish court, he enjoyed making observations in paint 'in which fantasy and invention have no limit'. Goya's haunting observation, opposite, was made at his home at Quinta del Sordo.

The Dog. Francisco de Goya. Spanish, 1746–1828

A very different kind of picture, and a very different kind of dog. Originating on the opposite side of the world, in China, these dogs were known poetically as 'butterfly lions' because they were as dainty as butterflies and as brave as the king of beasts. The frilled pet we see in the Japanese embroidery below is of course the Pekingese.

Pekingese Dog among Rose Petals. Japanese, *c.* 1900–15

There are many wonderful paintings of children with dogs, enough to fill volumes on their own. Below is a lovely detail from a large religious picture which the Venetian artist Paolo Veronese started in 1570 and took all of five years to complete. The girls, dressed in flowery taffeta, are Veronese's daughters, and the dog, who is bigger than either of them, is the family wolfhound. As one girl leans over to speak to the dog, her sister, with her mind on other things, props the pet up.

The famous painting opposite by the eighteenth-century English artist, Sir Joshua Reynolds, shows the pretty three-year-old Jane Bowles 'holding still' for her portrait while clasping her pet spaniel affectionately to her side.

Supper at Emmaus (detail). Paolo Veronese. Italian, c. 1528–88

Miss Bowles. Sir Joshua Reynolds. English 1723–92

The Cherry Tart. Pierre Bonnard. French, 1867–1947

It takes a few seconds before we notice the bright pair of eyes above the rim of the cherry tart, but then it's hard not to keep returning to them. Will the dog stare the tart off the table, or help himself to it, or will the girl reward him for his patience before it is too late? The French artist, Pierre Bonnard, loved painting tables of fruit and cakes out of doors – and animals too.

Three plump little puppies enjoying the happiest moment of the day. Apart from the interesting composition which balances the animals and the fruit on either side of a row of three goblets, it is the dogs that have always made this picture by Paul Gauguin especially popular. He painted it in 1888, three years before sailing from France to settle in Tahiti.

Still-life with Three Puppies. Paul Gauguin. French, 1848–1903

60

THE CATS HAVE COME TO TEA.

The Cats Have Come to Tea. Kate Greenaway. English, 1846–1901

While nearly everyone loves one breed of dog more than any other – long- or short-haired, hound, terrier or toy – most cat lovers, with fewer kinds to choose from, spread their love more equally over all.

In nineteenth-century England – when Kate Greenaway's enchanting cats came to tea, at left, and Edward Lear drew his own cat, Foss, below – cats were worshipped, not as sacred, of course, but as royal pets of the household. The most famous story of how great a hold cats can have over their mistresses is that of the Duchess of Richmond who willed a handsome sum of money to each of her many, many cats so she could die in peace knowing that one and all would receive the treatment of kings and queens, until they too passed on.

'When the tea is brought at five o'clock,
And all the neat curtains are drawn with care,
The little black cat with bright green eyes
Is suddenly purring there.'

Harold Monro
(*Milk for the Cat*)

Foss the Cat. Edward Lear.
English, 1812–88

As with dogs, no one can tell when cats were first domesticated. Cats were there at the beginning of history too.

In ancient Egypt, where the bronze creatures at left originated in 300 BC, the sacred cat Bast was worshipped as the goddess of music and pleasure.

Two Bronze Cats and Three Pottery Mice. Egyptian, Ptolemaic period, 304–30 BC (cats) and XII Dynasty, 1991–1786 BC (mice)

Reclining Cat, 1935. William Zorach. American, 1887–1966

In Japan, where the wooden cat with metal eyes, below, was carved, and in China where the cat up a tree – on the next page – was painted, superstition associated cats with the moon. It was even believed that cats possessed supernatural powers by which they could control the tides and the weather.

Cat. Japanese, 17th–18th cent.

When the American sculptor, William Zorach, created his *Reclining Cat* in 1935, he had no fairy-tale notions about cats personifying the moon, or of anything else but creating the plain, ordinary, beautiful, curled-up creature we see here.

The dogs have games written on their faces, but Pussy isn't having any. With claws sunk deep in the bark of the tree, the Chinese cat stares at the birds with bulging eyes. Likely as not he has climbed too close to the birds' nest for their comfort, so they must try to tempt – or frighten – him away.

Cat up a Tree. Chinese, 19th cent.

Spring Frolic in a T'ang Garden (detail). Chinese, Ch'ing Dynasty, 18th cent.

Hsüan Tsung, Emperor of China from 1426 to 1435, was an outstanding poet and calligrapher, and an exceptionally good artist besides. This enchanting kitten in a garden that might be said to be a Chinese cats' Eden – or Paradise – is believed to be a copy of one of Hsüan Tsung's delicate paintings.

Caretaker's Lodge. Robert Sivard. American, b. 1914

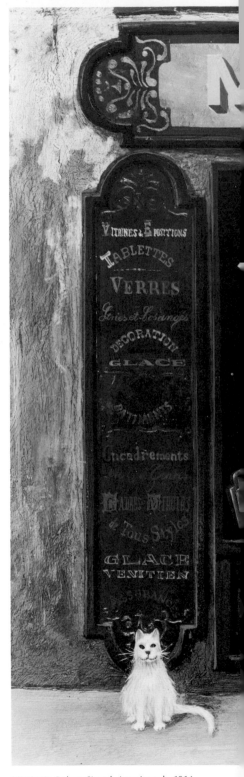

Miroiterie. Robert Sivard. American, b. 1914

For this French caretaker's cat, the window sill serves as a front-row balcony seat from which the passing show in the street below can be observed in peace and comfort.

By posing the boy and proud-looking cat almost the width of the shop apart, Robert Sivard invites us to window-shop in the charming and *very* French glazier's shop. Even though the shop only sells mirrors, it is easy to find ourselves trying to decide which kind of frame would suit the cat best, and which the portrait of the young boy.

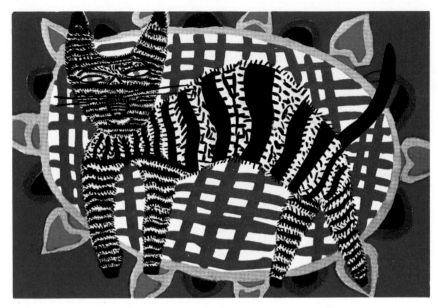

My Cat Awakes, 1952. Gabriella Granata. Italian, b. 1938

This tiger-striped cat belonged to a fourteen-year-old schoolgirl named Gabriella Granata, who saw her pet lying flat as a pattern in a basket. She has created a painting as bold and modern in feeling as a Matisse or a Miro.

A cat can also be a face. On a white circle, not unlike the puff of a cloud, two intense black dots

were painted in for the eyes and eight curving lines for the cat's whiskers. Although the picture is sometimes referred to as Joan Mirò's 'abstract' cat, the Spanish artist said that for him 'a form is never abstract, it is always a sign of something. It is always a man, a bird, or something else.'

The Cat's Whiskers. Joan Mirò. Spanish, b. 1893

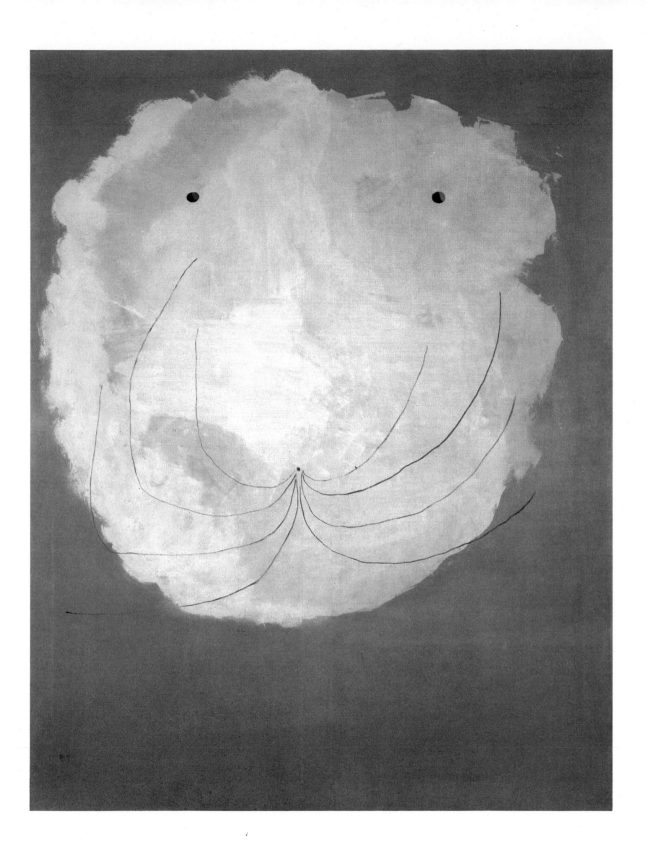

From the nineteenth century onward, almost as many paintings of children with cats are to be found as children with dogs – particularly in American folk art. But while portraying a *Girl with Cat*, Ammi Phillips couldn't resist the temptation of squeezing the dog in too.

Cats, birds, and cages. On the opposite page is Francisco de Goya's famous portrait of an elegant, innocent-looking young Spanish boy with his pet songbirds and three of the most purposeful-looking cats in eighteenth-century art. The magpie, or *Pica pica*, attached by a string round his left leg, holds a decorated card in his beak on which Goya has signed his name to the painting.

Girl in Red with her Cat and Dog. Ammi Phillips. American, 1787/8–1865

Don Manuel Osorio de Zuñiga. Francisco de Goya. Spanish, 1746–1828

The Language of the Birds. Habib Allah. Persian, *c.* 1600

Bunting and Lespedeza. Koyo. Japanese, c. 1830–50

Opposite is one of four miniatures, painted about 1600 by Habib Allah, for *The Language of the Birds*, a fable written four centuries earlier by the Persian poet, Farid al-din ʿAttar. The birds are assembled to discuss possible ways by which each could reach the Kingdom of God, or Paradise. Among them are the hoopoe, parakeet, crow, crane, grebe, heron, peacock and stork. The word 'Paradise' itself comes from a Persian word which means a royal park, or pleasure garden – perhaps more confined than this idyllic mountain scene, but hardly more beautiful.

A little bunting takes to the air from a flowering branch of lespedeza, or bush clover. One of the twelve lovely nineteenth-century paintings from Koyo's album of *Japanese Birds and Flowers*.

The most popular designs on pottery and china have always been birds and flowers. In this charming example, a bird decorates a blue and white tile from Holland.

Bird. Dutch, 17th cent.

'A bird of the air shall carry the voice, and that which hath wings shall tell the matter.'

Ecclesiastes 10:20

73

Opposite, a red bird of paradise is shown proudly displaying its handsome plumage with two very long and elegant tail wires. The print is from a natural history of birds published in Paris between 1796 and 1812. The artist, Jacques Barraband, is also noted for his bird decorations on Sèvres china.

This woodland creature, who loves creeping along the bark of trees on which it feeds, is a black and white warbler, one of the four hundred and thirty-five specimens John James Audubon painted for his monumental work, *The Birds of North America*, published between 1827 and 1839.

Black and White Warbler. John James Audubon. American, 1785–1851

Red Bird of Paradise. Jacques Barraband.
French, 1767–1809

Fantasy is the means whereby a plain ordinary cock can be made mysterious and poetic, as below, or delightfully cuckoo, as opposite.

Before moving to France in 1923, Marc Chagall was strongly influenced in his native Russia by the ballet. Yet while some of his famous floating, dancing, upside-down images, or the speeding *Red Rooster* below, may owe something to Russian ballet and folklore, mostly they are the direct result of the turnings of his highly individual mind.

The Red Rooster. Marc Chagall. Russian, b. 1887

Le Coq de Saché. Alexander Calder. American, 1898–1976

A few beer cans, coffee tins, a sardine-can opener, a little wire and lots of imagination resulted in Alexander Calder's airborne rooster. Calder divided his time between his native America, where the majority of his famed mobiles and stabiles are to be found, and France – hence the name of the French town, Saché, in the title of this fabulous creation.

Owl Scent Bottle. Greek, c. 650–625 BC

Saw-whet Owl. John James Audubon. American, 1785–1851

'Alone and warming his five wits,
The white owl in the belfry sits.'

Alfred, Lord Tennyson (*The Owl*)

Hecate (detail). William Blake. English, 1757–1827

Owls have always been popular, but never more so than they are today. One of the earliest known and most appealing examples of the owl in art is the Greek terracotta vessel, at left, made in the seventh century BC.

Owl Between Two Olive Branches. Greek, 5th cent. BC

Owl. French, 20th cent.

The most telling feature of this 'king of the night' is the size of his eyes, which can see in the dusk. The wise look of the owl greatly impressed the ancient Greeks, for whom it became the symbol of intelligence and wisdom.

Opposite, left, is the detail of a donkey and owl from William Blake's painting of Hecate, Greek goddess of witchcraft and of ghosts. To its right is an American saw-whet owl, drawn by John James Audubon.

The painting of an owl, above left, is from an ancient Greek pottery cup, and beside it is a young yet wise-looking twentieth-century owl as viewed by a child in France.

Elizabeth Ross (Mrs William Tyng). John Singleton Copley. American, 1738–1815

Venus Drawn by Doves. American, early 19th cent.

'And there my little dove did sit With feathers softly brown.'

E. B. Browning (*My Doves*)

The dove has always symbolized peace, purity and gentleness. It was the dove which Noah sent out from the ark to report on the level of the waters, and which came circling back holding the olive branch in its beak; and it is the dove that was chosen in Christian art to represent the Holy Spirit.

The dove was held sacred to Venus, the goddess of love and beauty, who is to be seen at right, being drawn across a New England sky by a *very* large pair of them. This enchanting folk picture, which combines painting and cut paper on silk, was discovered in Massachusetts.

Above: In introducing the dove, as a symbol of purity, into his formal portrait of sixteen-year-old Elizabeth Ross of Maine, the Boston painter John Singleton Copley was following a tradition dating back to ancient Greece.

And this is the bold and lively way Ben Shahn drew a dove in 1949.

Turtle Dove. Ben Shahn. American, b. (Russia) 1898

Circe. Dosso Dossi. Italian, d. 1542

Comus with the Lady Spellbound. William Blake. English, 1757–1827

A place very far from Paradise was the legendary island of Aeaea, belonging to the beautiful Circe, daughter of the Sun. According to the story in the adventures of Ulysses, the creatures here were once humans who, after being lured to these shores by Circe's sweet songs and wined and dined by the enchantress, were transformed into animals and birds as she touched them with her magic wand.

Magic also plays a major part in the masque which John Milton wrote about Circe's son, Comus, the god of mirth and revelry. William Blake shows Comus with his magic rod, tempting the Lady seated in the enchanted chair to drink from his magic cup. Had she done so she would at once have been transformed into an animal – as were the unfortunate merry-makers at the banquet table directly behind her.

Lion. Artist unknown. Chinese, Ch'ien Lung period, 1736–1796

The fabulous dragon, born entirely of the human imagination, has been almost anything grotesque that artists have wanted to make it. A dragon can be the guardian of Paradise, and an omen of good, as in ancient China where it became a symbol of creativity and the sign of a good harvest. It can be the symbol of evil, too: a monster to be overcome by a hero or by a saint.

Opposite is an illustration Kay Nielsen made in 1925 for the Grimm Brothers' ancient fairy tale, 'The Two Brothers'. This is the moment when the dragon threatens the young hunter: 'many a knight has already left his life behind him, and you I will kill dead as they'.

To western eyes, the fanciful jewel-like beast above, created by an eighteenth-century Chinese artist, looks almost as much like a dragon as it does a lion.

Rhino Wolf (detail). Attributed to Sultan Muhammed. Persian, mid 16th cent.

At right, the dragon-like monster, whose ferocity is softened by a delightfully decorative face, is a detail from one of Sultan Muhammed's miniatures for the *Shah Nameh*, or Book of Kings, painted in Persia in the sixteenth century.

Dragon. Kay Nielsen. Danish, 1886–1957

The paintings of Hieronymus Bosch, 'the greatest master of fantasy', abound with beauty and strangeness. Familiar animals such as giraffes, elephants, hogs and hounds share his landscapes with the oddest companions like the weird creatures here who occupy a small area of his large painting, *The Garden of Delights*.

A Peruvian potter's answer to Hieronymus Bosch. The grey bird-like jar, when blown into at the tail end, whistles at the other.

The Garden of Delights (detail). Hieronymus Bosch. Dutch, c. 1450–1516

Whistling Jar. Peruvian, 1000–1476 AD

'The ivory framework of the limbs so light
Moved like a pair of balances deflected,
There glided through the coat a gleam of white,
And on the forehead, where the beams collected,
Stood, like a moon-lit tower, the horn so bright,
At every footstep proudly re-erected.'

Rainer Maria Rilke (*The Unicorn*)

The most spiritual of the mythical animals – the
creatures that might have been but never were – is
the unicorn. Legend has it that no animal could
overtake him, no hunter capture him, but when
confronted by a maiden the unicorn would lay his
head on her lap and thus become tamed. In the
fifteenth century, this creature of great gentleness
and mystery became the symbol of purity and
eternal rebirth.

Unicorns. Arthur B. Davies. American, 1862–1928

A horse with a long horn rising from its brow, with
the beard of a goat and the tail of a lion. The captive
unicorn at left, resting beneath a pomegranate tree
to which it is attached by a chain of gold, is the final
scene in a magnificent series of medieval tapestries
depicting the *Unicorn Hunt*. The scenes have been
interpreted as representing the death and
resurrection of Christ.

Unicorn Hunt (detail of tapestry series).
French or Flemish, *c.* 1500

In our own century, the American artist Arthur B. Davies, who enjoyed letting his imagination take wing, painted this hauntingly beautiful dream landscape in which no less than three of the whitest unicorns appear.

Hieronymus Bosch included this lovely detail of a unicorn sharing a drink with other animals in *The Garden of Delights*. Another detail from the same painting appears on pages 86–87.

Garden of Delights (detail). Hieronymus Bosch.
Dutch, c. 1450–1516

Animal Scroll. Toba Sojo. Japanese, 12th cent.

As well as imagining fantastic animals such as the dragon and the unicorn, artists have taken ordinary, everyday animals and pictured them as humans. Perhaps the start of it all was the strange image of a man with a head of a bird, discovered in a three-thousand-year-old Egyptian tomb. Then there was Aesop whose fables gave the spinners of fairy tales many entertaining ideas. On these and the following pages familiar animals are seen acting as we do – more or less.

An ass teaching grammar to a class of young parrots – one nursing a toothache – is but one of two hundred delights in

Grandville's *Album des bêtes*. The book was published in France in 1864, and – no wonder – has influenced children's book illustration ever since.

What could look more natural than these animals up to the same high jinks as children? The scene,

above, from a twelfth-century scroll by the Japanese artist, Toba Sojo, is among the best caricatures of the kind ever done.

are ferrets! Where _can_ I have dropped them, I wonder?" Alice guessed in a moment that it was looking for the nosegay and the pair of white kid gloves, and she began hunting for them, but they were now nowhere to be seen— everything seemed to have changed since her swim in the pool, and her walk along the river-bank with its fringe of rushes and forget-me-nots, and the glass table and the little door had vanished.

Soon the rabbit noticed Alice, as she stood looking curiously about her, and at once said in a quick angry tone, "why, Mary Ann! what are _you_ doing out here? Go home this moment, and look on my dressing-table for my gloves and nosegay, and fetch them here, as quick as you can run, do you hear?" and Alice was so much frightened that she ran off at once, without

Alice and the White Rabbit. Lewis Carroll. English, 1832–98

The White Rabbit with Alice in 'Alice's Adventures Under Ground', the story Lewis Carroll wrote for the young Alice Liddell in 1862. Three years later the book had developed into *Alice's Adventures in Wonderland*, printed not with the author's sketches but with John Tenniel's illustrations, such as the familiar White Rabbit below.

Ass Giving Lesson on the French Verb 'Ennuyer': To Bore. Jean-Ignace Grandville. French, 1803–47

The White Rabbit. Sir John Tenniel. English, 1820–1914

The Daw in Borrowed Plumes, opposite, is one of the twenty illustrations Charles H. Bennett made in 1857 for a rare English edition of Aesop's *Fables*. Here we see the rich and vulgar jackdaw who had a mind to be genteel, 'tricked out' in all the gay feathers which fell from the fashionable peacocks. By common consent the indignant peacocks fell upon the Daw and snatched back their plumes. 'Fine feathers', Aesop was the first to say, 'do not always make fine birds.'

Daw in Borrowed Plumes. Charles H. Bennett. English, 1828–67

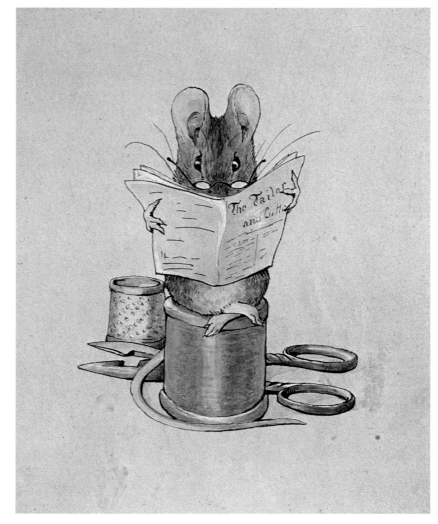

The Tailor Mouse. Beatrix Potter. English, 1866–1943

Rabbit Doctor. Detail from a Book of Hours. French, 15th cent.

It is Beatrix Potter's magic that makes this spectacled mouse, seated with feet crossed on a spool of thread and intently reading his newspaper, look so natural – and so charming. He is the principal character in *The Tailor of Gloucester*, the second of Beatrix Potter's many books, and the one *she* liked the most.

The rabbit, at left, gathering herbs for medicine, is an animal doctor in a fifteenth-century French prayerbook or Book of Hours.

93

And what could be more cat-like – yet human – more modern and enchanting than Saul Steinberg's portrait of four proud creatures whose ancestors without question must have shared the Garden of Eden with ours?

Cats. Saul Steinberg. American, b. (Romania) 1914

ARTISTS AND ILLUSTRATIONS

ARTISTS UNKNOWN

Raven Addressing Assembled Animals. British Museum, London. 2.

Giraffe and Elephant. Neolithic rock engraving (palimpsest). Found at Habeter III, Fezzan, North Africa. Photo Frobenius Institut, Frankfurt. 10.

Water Buffalo. Minneapolis Institute of Arts. Bequest of Alfred F. Pillsbury. 11.

Cheetahs. British Museum, London. 11.

Elephant. Freer Gallery of Art, Washington D.C. 14.

Elephant Armour. H.M. Tower of London. Reproduced by permission of Her Majesty's Stationery Office. 14.

Escaping Elephant. British Museum, London. 15.

Bear in a Tree. National Gallery of Art, Washington D.C. Gift of Edgar William and Bernice Chrysler Garbisch. 16–17.

Three Bear Cubs. Courtesy, Museum of Fine Arts, Boston. Francis Bartlett Donation. 18.

Squirrels on a Branch. Courtesy the Estate of the late Dr Schapiro. 20–21.

Rabbit with Figs. Photo Scala. 22.

Falling Mountain Goat. Pierpont Morgan Library, New York. 26–27.

Goat Statuette. Courtesy, Museum of Fine Arts, Boston. 27.

Goat Weathervane. Smithsonian Institution, Washington D.C. Eleanor and Mabel van Alstyne American Folk Art Collection. 27.

Bahram Gur and Azada Just Before the Hunt. Miniature from *Khamseh* (Book IV, Eight Paradises) by Mir Khusrau Dihlavi. Metropolitan Museum of Art, New York. Gift of Alexander Smith Cochran, 1913. 29.

Bull Rhyton. District Museum of History, Borovo, Rousse District, Bulgaria. 30.

Bull and Bird, pottery bowl. British Museum, London. 31.

Pageant Sleigh, Representing a Stag Hunt. Metropolitan Museum of Art, New York. Rogers Fund. 37.

Porky with Rider Up. Collection Mr and Mrs Peter H. Tillou. 39.

Departure from China. Episode 2 from the Chinese handscroll: *Eighteen Songs of a Nomad Flute*. Metropolitan Museum of Art, New York. Gift of the Dillon Fund. 40–41.

Chariot. Mycenaean krater. Metropolitan Museum of Art, New York. Cesnola Collection, purchased by subscription, 1874–76. 43.

Colossal Marble Horse from Halikarnassos (fragment). British Museum, London. 46.

Four Horses, Concentric Design. Courtesy, Museum of Fine Arts, Boston. Francis Bartlett Donation. 46.

Equestrian Portrait of a Prince. Metropolitan Museum of Art, New York. 47.

Donkey Nursing Lion Cubs. Courtesy, Museum of Fine Arts, Boston. 50.

Pekingese Dog among Rose Petals. Kalamazoo Public Museum. A.M. Todd Collection. 57.

Two Bronze Cats and Three Pottery Mice. Metropolitan Museum of Art, New York. Theodore M. Davis Collection and Carnarvon Collection. 63.

Cat. Private collection. 63.

Cat up a Tree. Author's collection. 64.

Bird. Polychrome tile. 'De Lakenhal' Museum, Leiden. 73.

Owl Scent Bottle. Terracotta. Louvre, Paris. Photo Giraudon. 78.

Owl Between Two Olive Branches. Worcester Art Museum, Massachusetts. Gift of Mrs Penelope S. Canfield. 79.

Owl. Child's drawing. 79.

Venus Drawn by Doves. Abby Aldrich Rockefeller Folk Art Center, Williamsburg, Virginia. 81.

Lion. Porcelain figure. Metropolitan Museum of Art, New York. Bequest of Benjamin Altman, 1913. 84.

Spring Frolic in a T'ang Garden (detail). After Hsüan Tsung. Metropolitan Museum of Art, New York. Fletcher Fund, 1947. 65.

Whistling Jar. The Metropolitan Museum of Art, New York. Crosby Brown Collection of Musical Instruments, 1889. 86.

Unicorn. Detail from the Unicorn Hunt tapestry series, number 7, from the Château of Verteuil.

Metropolitan Museum of Art, New York. Cloisters Collection. Gift of John D. Rockefeller, Jr., 1937. 88.

Choju Giga (Animal Scroll). Kozan-ji Temple, Kyoto, Japan. 90.

Rabbit Doctor. Pierpont Morgan Library, New York. 93.

ALLAH, HABIB *The Concourse of the Birds*. Miniature from Farid-al-din 'Attar (1119—1230): *Mantiq-al-Tayr (The Language of the Birds)*. Metropolitan Museum of Art, New York, Fletcher Fund, 1963. 72.

AUDUBON, JOHN JAMES *Fox Squirrels*. From *Quadrupeds of North America*, 1854. 20.

Head of a Buffalo Calf. Private collection. 31.

Black and White Warbler. From *Birds of America*, 1827–38. 75.

Saw-Whet Owl. From *Birds of America*, 1827–38. 78.

BACON, PEGGY *The Ineluctable Caller*. Private collection. 38.

BARRABAND, JACQUES *Red Bird of Paradise*. From François Lavillant: *Histoire naturelle des oiseaux*, 1796–1812. 74.

BASSANO, JACOPO, Studio of. *The Animals Going into the Ark*. Reproduced by Gracious Permission of Her Majesty Queen Elizabeth The Queen Mother. 6–7.

BENNETT, CHARLES H. *Daw in Borrowed Plumes*. Pierpont Morgan Library, New York. 92.

BLAKE, WILLIAM *Adam Naming the Beasts*. Glasgow Art Galleries and Museums, Stirling Maxwell Collection, Pollok House. 6.

Hecate (detail). Tate Gallery, London. 78.

Comus with the Lady Spellbound. H.E. Huntington Library, San Marino, California. 83.

BONNARD, PIERRE *The Cherry Tart*. Galerie Nathan, Zurich. 60.

BOSCH, HIERONYMUS *The Garden of Delights*, triptych (left wing). Prado, Madrid. Photo Scala. 86–87, 89.

CALDER, ALEXANDER *Sow*. Museum of Modern Art, New York. 39.

Le Coq de Saché. Private collection. 77.

CARROLL, LEWIS (Charles Lutwidge Dodgson) *Alice and the White Rabbit*. British Library, London (Add. ms. 46700, f.18). 91.

CHAGALL, MARC *The Red Rooster*. Cincinnati Art Museum.

Bequest of Mary E. Johnston, 1967. 76.

COPLEY, JOHN SINGLETON *Elizabeth Ross (Mrs William Tyng)*. Courtesy, Museum of Fine Arts, Boston. M. and M. Karolik Collection. 80.

DAVIES, ARTHUR B. *Unicorns*. Metropolitan Museum of Art, New York. Bequest of Lillie P. Bliss, 1931. 88–89.

DEGAS, EDGAR *Rearing Horse*. Bronze statuette. Private collection. 51.

DOSSI, DOSSO *Circe*. National Gallery of Art, Washington D.C. 82–83.

DÜRER, ALBRECHT *Hare*. Albertina, Vienna. 22.

FIELD, ERASTUS SALISBURY *The Garden of Eden*. Courtesy, Museum of Fine Arts, Boston. M. and M. Karolik Collection. 4.

FLANNAGAN, JOHN B. *Chimpanzee*. Whitney Museum of American Art, New York. 24.

FRINK, L.W. *The Buffalo of the Plains*. Private collection. 31.

GAUGUIN, PAUL *Still-life with Three Puppies*. The Museum of Modern Art, New York. Mrs Simon Guggenheim Fund. 61.

GÉRICAULT, THÉODORE *Head of a White Horse*. Louvre, Paris. Photo Réunion des Musées Nationaux. 45.

GOYA, FRANCISCO DE *The Dog*. Prado, Madrid. Photo Mas. 56.

Don Manuel Osorio de Zuñiga. Metropolitan Museum of Art, New York. Jules S. Bache Collection, 1949. 77.

GRANATA, GABRIELLA *My Cat Awakes*. Private collection. 68.

GRANDVILLE, JEAN IGNACE ISIDORE GÉRARD *Ass Giving Lesson on French Verb 'Ennuyer': To Bore*. From *Album des bêtes*. 90.

GREENAWAY, KATE *The Cats Have Come to Tea*. From *Marigold Garden. Pictures and Rhymes*, 1885. 62.

GUYS, CONSTANTIN *The Calash*. Private collection. 43.

HICKS, EDWARD *The Peaceable Kingdom*. Worcester Art Museum, Massachusetts. 8.

The Peaceable Kingdom (detail). Metropolitan Museum of Art, New York. Gift of Edgar William and Bernice Chrysler Garbisch, 1970. 8–9.

HSÜAN TSUNG. See ARTIST

UNKNOWN, *Spring Frolic in a T'ang Garden*. 65.

KIOSAI, KAWANABE *Monkeys in Fruit Tree*. From *Book of Humorous Drawings*, 1881. Victoria and Albert Museum, London. 24–25.

KOYO *Bunting and Lespedeza*. From album *Japanese Birds and Flowers*, British Museum, London. 73.

LEAR, EDWARD *Foss the Cat*. Sketch from letter written to Emily Tennyson, 1876. Tennyson Research Centre, Lincoln. Photo, Lincolnshire Library Service. 62.

LEE, DORIS *Mare with Mule Colts*. Photo Midtown Gallery, New York. 50–51.

LOUFF, CHARLES. See MURPHY. 52.

MATISSE, HENRI *Rabbits*. Private collection. 23.

MIRÒ, JOAN *The Cat's Whiskers*. From the collection of Mr and Mrs Burton-Tremaine, Meriden, Connecticut. 69.

MUHAMMED, SULTAN (attributed to) *A Camel with his Driver*. Private collection. 11.

Rhino Wolf. Detail of *Bahram Gur Slays the Rhino Wolf*, miniature from Firdowsi: *Shah-nameh (Book of Kings)*. Made for Shah Tahmasp (reigned 1524–76). Metropolitan Museum of Art, New York. Gift of Arthur A. Houghton, Jr., 1970. 84.

MURPHY, CHARLES *Carousel Horse*. Painting after carving by Charles Louff. National Gallery of Art, Washington D.C. Index of American Design. 52.

NIELSEN, KAY *Dragon*, 1925. From Brothers Grimm: *The Two Brothers*, 1925. 85.

PALIZZI, FILIPPO *The Calf*. Galleria Nazionale di Arte Moderna, Rome. Photo Alinari. 34.

PHILLIPS, AMMI *Girl in Red with her Cat and Dog*. Private collection. 70.

PICASSO, PABLO *Drop-curtain for 'Parade'*. Musée National d'Art Moderne, Paris. Photo Réunion des Musées Nationaux. 53.

PISANELLO, ANTONIO *Horse*. Study. Louvre, Paris. Photo Bulloz. 42.

POTTER, BEATRIX *The Tailor Mouse*. From *The Tailor of Gloucester*, 1903, published by Frederick Warne, London. Tate Gallery, London. Photo John Webb. 93.

RAGINI, TODI *Woman Standing Beside a Pool*. Courtesy, Museum of Fine Arts, Boston. Gift of John Goelet. 28.

REMBRANDT VAN RIJN. *The Polish Rider*. Copyright The Frick Collection, New York. 44–45.

REMMICK, JOSEPH *Pig Toy*. Private

collection. 39.

REYNOLDS, SIR JOSHUA *Miss Bowles*. Trustees of the Wallace Collection, London. 59.

RICE, WILLIAM *Goodwin Tavern Sign*. Wadsworth Atheneum, Hartford, Connecticut. 12.

ROUSSEAU, HENRI *The Sleeping Gypsy*. The Museum of Modern Art, New York. Gift of Mrs Simon Guggenheim. 12–13.

Monsieur Juniet's Carriage. Private collection. Photo Giraudon. 36–37.

RUBENS, PETER PAUL *The Farm at Laeken*. Reproduced by Gracious Permission of Her Majesty The Queen. 32–33.

SCOTT-LEIGHTON, NICHOLAS WINFIELD *The Young Aristocrat*. Addison Gallery of American Art, Phillips Academy, Andover, Massachusetts. 37.

SESSHU *Monkeys and Birds in Trees* (detail). Courtesy, Museum of Fine Arts, Boston. 24.

SHAHN, BEN *Turtle Dove*. From *A Partridge in a Pear Tree*, published by The Museum of Modern Art, New York, 1964. 80.

SIVARD, ROBERT *Caretaker's Lodge*. Private collection. 66.

Miroiterie. Midtown Galleries, New York. 66–67.

STEEN, JAN *The Poultry Yard* (detail). Mauritshuis, The Hague. 35.

STEINBERG, SAUL *Cats*. Private collection. 94.

STEVENS, EDWARD JOHN *Three Koalas*. Courtesy, The Weyhe Gallery, New York. 19.

STUBBS, GEORGE *Prince of Wales's Phaeton*. Reproduced by Gracious Permission of Her Majesty The Queen. 48–49.

TENNIEL, SIR JOHN *The White Rabbit*. From Lewis Carroll: *Alice's Adventures in Wonderland*, 1865. British Museum, London. Photo Freeman. 91.

TOULOUSE-LAUTREC, HENRI DE *Clown, Pony and Monkey Rider*. Art Institute of Chicago. 54.

Follette. Philadelphia Museum of Art. 55.

Woman Driving a Carriage and Pair. Sketchbook drawing. Art Institute of Chicago. Robert Alexander Waller Memorial Fund, 1949. 55.

VERONESE, PAOLO *Supper at Emmaus* (detail). Louvre, Paris. Photo Giraudon. 58.

WARNECKE, HEINZ *Tumbling Bears*. Whitney Museum of American Art, New York. 19.

YEE, CHIANG *Mao Mao the Giant Panda*. From Chiang Yee: *Chin Pao and the Giant Pandas*, 1939. 17.

ZORACH, WILLIAM *Reclining Cat*. Private collection. 63.